A New Series Of Designs For Ornamental Cottages And Villas: With Estimates Of The Probable Cost Of Erecting Them

Peter Frederick Robinson

A NEW SERIES OF DESIGNS

FOR

ORNAMENTAL COTTAGES AND VILLAS,

WITH

ESTIMATES OF THE PROBABLE COST OF ERECTING THEM;

FORMING A SEQUEL TO THE WORKS ENTITLED

RURAL ARCHITECTURE

AND

DESIGNS FOR ORNAMENTAL VILLAS.

BY

P. F. ROBINSON,

ARCHITECT, F.A.S. F.G.S. AND VICE PRESIDENT OF THE INSTITUTE OF BRITISH ARCHITECTS;
AUTHOR OF A WORK ON RURAL ARCHITECTURE; DESIGNS FOR ORNAMENTAL VILLAS; FARM
BUILDINGS; VILLAGE ARCHITECTURE; LODGES AND PARK ENTRANCES;
DOMESTIC ARCHITECTURE; AND THE VITRUVIUS BRITANNICUS.

———◆———

FIFTY-SIX PLATES.

THE LANDSCAPES DRAWN ON STONE BY J. D. HARDING AND T. ALLOM.

———◆———

LONDON:
HENRY G. BOHN, 4, YORK STREET, COVENT GARDEN.
MDCCCXXXVIII.

ADDRESS.

My former work on Rural Architecture having passed through four editions, and having been generally received with much favour; I am induced to publish a New Series, consisting of buildings already executed, or now in progress. Two of these designs arise from alterations made in old buildings, and it may be observed, that good effects are frequently produced by such alterations, at a very moderate expense, and that Cottages especially may be rendered attractive by a judicious improvement of the form, as regards doors, windows, and chimnies. This, however, requires the hand of experience, and cannot be effected by a mere workman. It is like the last touches given to a picture by the hand of the master, and requires delicacy and feeling in the application. The improvement which has taken place, during the last ten years, in our Rural Architecture, is very evident; and it is pleasing to observe the interest which this humble but attractive pursuit excites. When good effects can be produced at a moderate expense, and the scenery of our native country embellished by improving the condition of the peasantry, the work may be considered truly national.

The first Eight Designs, comprehending the Smithy, the School House, the Gate Cottage, the Cottage, the Farm House, the Mill, and two Cottages on a very economical scale, may be considered a continuation of my work on Rural Architecture; the remaining Six Designs to that entitled Ornamental Villas.

P. F. ROBINSON.

BROOK STREET, GROSVENOR SQUARE,
March 1, 1838.

A LIST OF THE PLATES

in the

NEW SERIES

of

DESIGNS FOR ORNAMENTAL COTTAGES,

FORMING THE FIRST DIVISION OF THIS VOLUME.

LIST OF THE PLATES.

A LIST OF THE PLATES

IN THE

NEW SERIES

OF

DESIGNS FOR ORNAMENTAL VILLAS,

FORMING THE SECOND DIVISION OF THIS VOLUME.

ORNAMENTAL COTTAGES.

DESIGN, No. I.

THE Smithy in village scenery has always been a favourite subject with the scenic Draughtsman, and a little aid from the Architect may render it still more so. The building, explained by the Plates 1, 2, 3, 4, has recently been erected at Prestwood, near Stourbridge, in Worcestershire, and the spot is peculiarly beautiful. A small dwelling is attached to the Smithy, and the whole groupes well. A similar building may be erected, for £350, including all the outbuildings. The Cottage alone might be built for £150.

Smithy

Parlour

Yard

Outhouse

Dairy

Kitchen

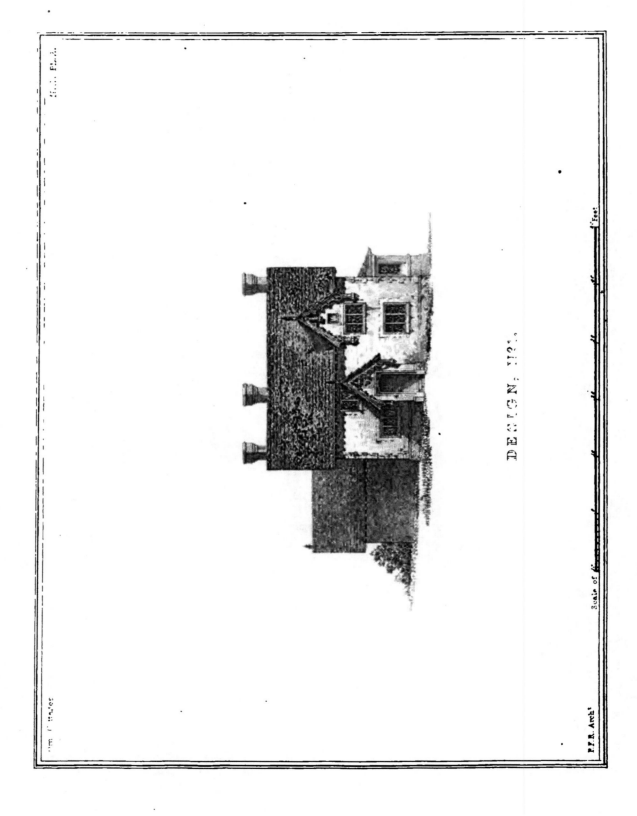

DESIGN, N° 12.

Scale of _____ Feet

F.F.R. Archt

Plan Cottage.

P.F.R. Archton. delin.

Printed by Chaloux et al.

ORNAMENTAL COTTAGES.

DESIGN, No. II.

THE School House must at all times be an object of interest, as it is frequently visited by its patrons. It should be kept with great care, as the health of the children must depend upon a well-arranged system of cleanliness. Some attention as to picturesque effect in the construction of the building, will add to the attraction, particularly when the scenery is good. The Design, No. 2, the subject of Plates 5, 6, 7, 8, is in progress at Prestwood, and it is intended to use the building occasionally as a Chapel, the partitions dividing the School-rooms, from the Mistresses-room being moveable. Each School-room provides sufficient space for ninety children, and a small Shed between each, is furnished with a Pump, and a Sink for washing. The estimate amounts to £420.

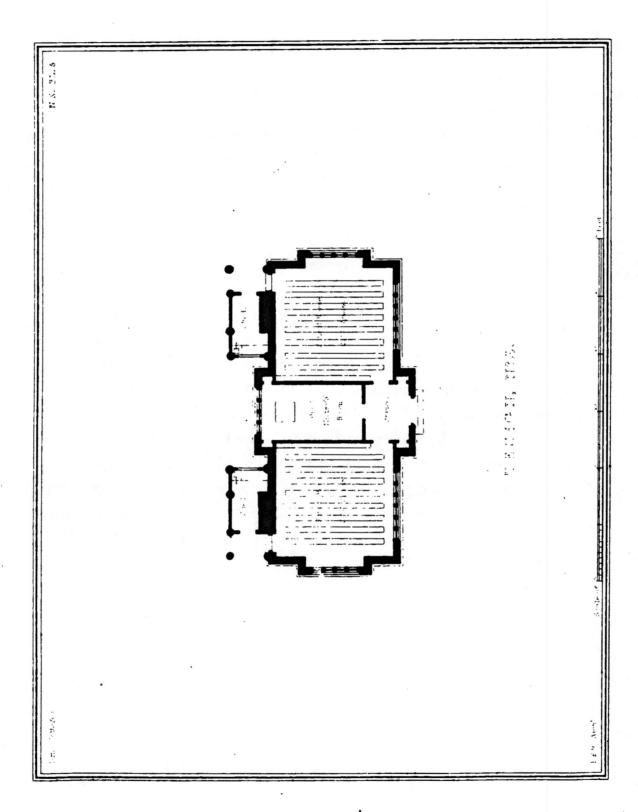

Orm. Cottages.

J.F.A. drn' Constone in I. Allens.

Printed by C. Hulmandels.

DESIGN N9 2.

ORNAMENTAL COTTAGES.

DESIGN, No. III.

THE Gate Lodge (see Plates 9, 10, 11, 12), provides for two families, comprehending a Parlour, thirteen feet by eleven, and a Kitchen of the same size, in each, with four Chambers above. The original building is old, but some scenic effect has been given, by improving the shape of the Doors and Windows, the Gables and Chimnies. The Porch and Awning have also been added. Cottage buildings in general may be improved in this manner, at a moderate expense, but great care and attention is necessary in making such additions. A Lodge of this description may be erected for £300.

N.S. Pl. 1.

P.F.R. Arch.

Scale of ___ Feet.

Orn Cottages

P.F.R Archt m.Dorc by T.Allom

Printed by C Hullmandel

DESIGN N.24.

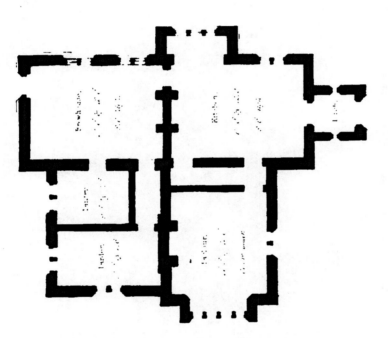

P.F.R Arch.

DESIGN N°. 6.

cm Cottages

P.F.R. Arch. on stone by C. Haase

Printed by C. Hullmandel.

DESIGN Nº 4.

ORNAMENTAL COTTAGES.

DESIGN, No. V.

THE Farm House (Plates 17, 18, 19, 20), is now in progress at Prestwood. It comprehends a Kitchen, seventeen feet by sixteen feet; a Parlour, thirteen feet by twelve feet; a Brew-house, seventeen feet by fourteen feet; with a Dairy and Pantry; to which is attached a Saddler's Shop, twelve feet by ten feet; and a Grocer's Shop, twelve feet by ten feet; as the Farmer carries on both these occupations. On the Bed Chamber Story are five Rooms. The building is of some size, and the situation is picturesque. The expense will amount to about £700.

Oan Cottages

F. M. Arch'

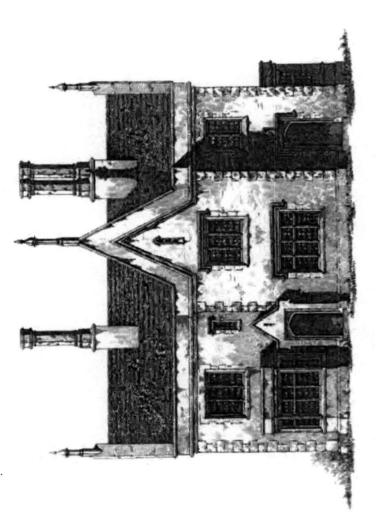

DESIGN No. 5.

Cow Cottage.

P F R. Arch.! on Stone by T. Allom.

Printed by C. Hullmandel.

DESIGN Nº 6.

ORNAMENTAL COTTAGES.

DESIGN, No. VI.

THE Mill House frequently becomes a subject of pictorial interest, and by a little management in planting, or in opening a vista, much may be excited. The subject of the present Design (Plates 21, 22, 23, 24), is an old building, used as a Rolling Mill, and the object has been to create some effect, by improving the form of the Windows, Doors, Chimnies, &c. As the Elevation, Plate 23, is seen from the pleasure-ground walks, the appearance of an ancient Chapel has been attempted, and the effect is not unpleasing. The expense attending the alteration of this building (originally very ugly), has been trifling.

DESIGN, Nᵒ 35.

DESIGN No. 6.

Orn. Cottages

DESIGN No. 33.

Scale of

PFR Archt

Feet

N.S. Pl.24.

Orn. Cottages

F.P.R. Arch. drawn on stone by E. Blore.

Printed by C. Hullmandel.

DESIGN Nº 6.

ORNAMENTAL COTTAGES.

DESIGN, No. VII.

THE Design, No. 7, is a Cottage upon a very small scale, arranged with a view to economy in every respect, simple in form, but possessing some features so as to render it pleasing. In improving Estates it is desirable to adopt a plan which shall afford shelter to the labourer, and such comforts as a humble dwelling of this description can produce. It frequently happens that Cottages are erected without much regard to plan, but every thing depends upon the relative situation of Doors and Windows, or the poor man's habitation will be rendered comfortless. This Cottage comprehends a Kitchen, twelve feet by ten feet; a Bed Chamber, eight feet by seven feet, which is merely large enough to contain a bed, a table and chair; and an Outhouse, eight feet by seven feet, and a Pantry. The expense would not exceed £100.

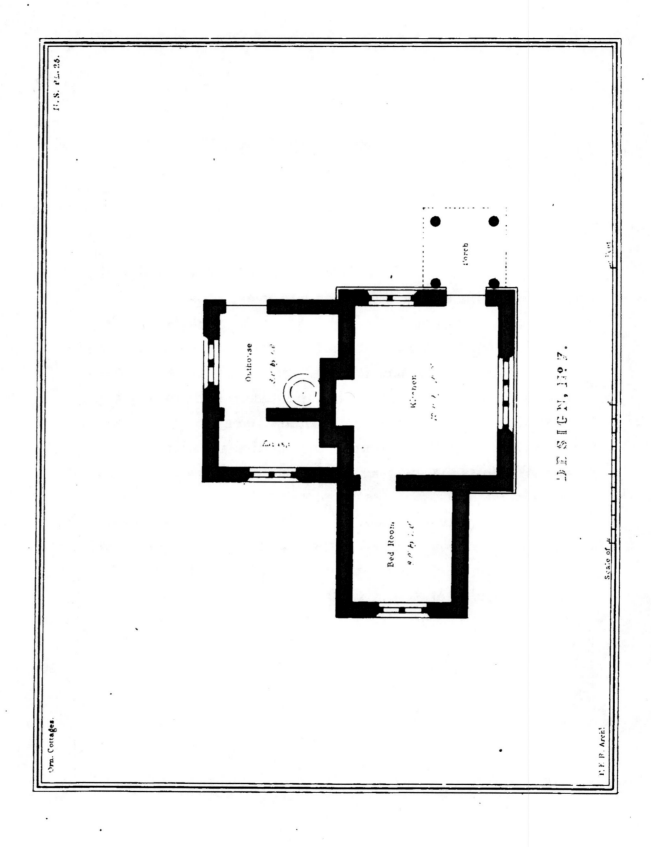

DESIGN, No. 7.

Out House

Kitchen

Bed Room

Porch

Scale of

DESIGN, N.º 7.

P. F. R. Arch.

Scale of Feet

Orn. Cottages.

DESIGN, 107.

P. F. R. Arch.t

Scale of _____ Feet

Drawn by J. Harding

Designed by P.F.R.

Printed by C.Hullmandel

DESIGN, &c.

ORNAMENTAL COTTAGES.

DESIGN, No. VIII.

THE Design, No. 8, has been studied so as to produce the smallest building in which a human being could be placed. The Kitchen measures ten feet by nine feet; the Bed Room nine feet by seven feet, and the Outhouse ten feet by six feet. It might be erected for £100., or under favourable circumstances for something less.

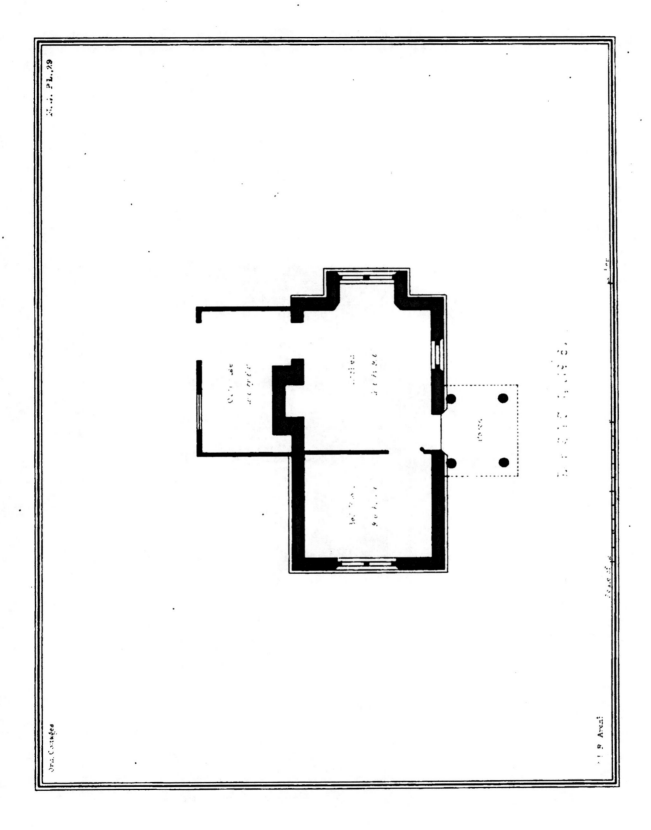

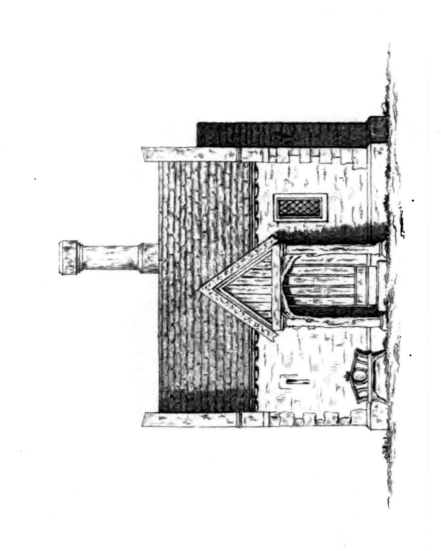

COTTAGE

Chro. Collinger

Drawn by J D Harding

DESIGN N° 7.

Designed by P.F.R.

Printed by C.Hullmandel

'A Vautier lithog

ORNAMENTAL VILLAS.

NEW SERIES.

DESIGN, No. I.

BINSWOOD Cottage at Leamington in Warwickshire was erected in the year 1824 for Edward Willes, Esq. from the Author's Designs, and under his superintendence. It is well known to the visitors of that place, but has now lost much of its attraction in consequence of the increased number of new buildings surrounding it. It is a Villa upon a small scale, in the Cottage style, consisting of a Porch entrance and Staircase; a Drawing Room twenty-two feet by fifteen; a Vestibule opening into the Garden, sixteen feet by ten feet; and a Dining Room twenty-two feet by fifteen. Kitchen, Scullery, Larders, &c. to which Stabling has since been added. The Chamber Story contains six Rooms, with Groom's Room over the Stabling. It is built of brick, and stuccoed in imitation of stone, and might now be erected for £2,500.

DESIGN. No 1.

Drawing Room

Dining Room

Kitchen

Vestibule

Larder

Scullery

Porch

Staircase

DESIGN, No 1.

Gen View

PER Arch   Scale of

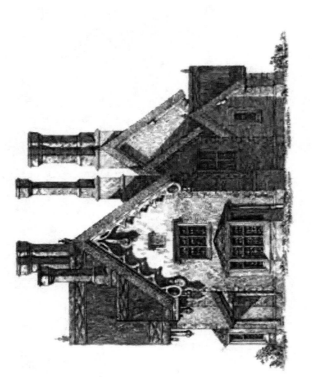

DESIGN, No 1.

Scale of Feet

E.F.R. Arch.

Own Villas

Drawn by J.E. Harding

W.Winter-lithog.

DESIGN. No.

Designed by P.F.R.

Printed by Hullmandel

ORNAMENTAL VILLAS.

NEW SERIES.

DESIGN, No. II.

THE Plates 5, 6, 7, 8, are descriptive of a building on the estate of H. H. Foley, Esq. at Prestwood, near Stourbridge. It is now used as a Farm House, but would be applicable as a small Villa. It consists of an Entrance Porch; an Eating Room, sixteen feet six inches by thirteen feet; a Drawing Room of the same size; a Study, thirteen feet by nine feet; a Store Room, thirteen feet by nine feet; a Kitchen, eighteen feet by thirteen feet; Scullery, Larder, and Servants' Hall. The upper Story contains five best Bed Chambers, and three Servants' Rooms. The original building not having been very attractive, some alterations and additions have been made, with a view to improve its appearance. It might be erected for the sum of £2,500.

Servants Hall

Own Room

Store Room

Drawing Room

Pantry

Scullery

Kitchen

House keepers Room

Dining Room

Porch

DESIGN No 55

Scale of

P E R Arch

Feet

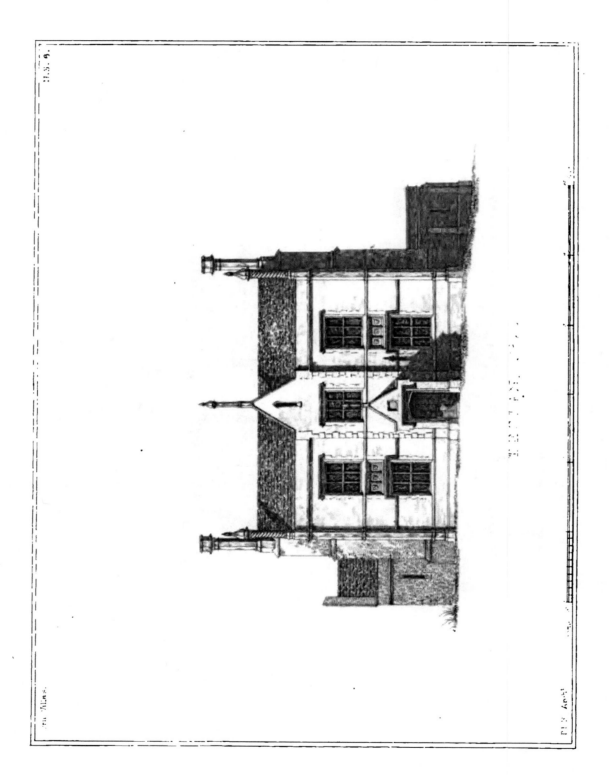

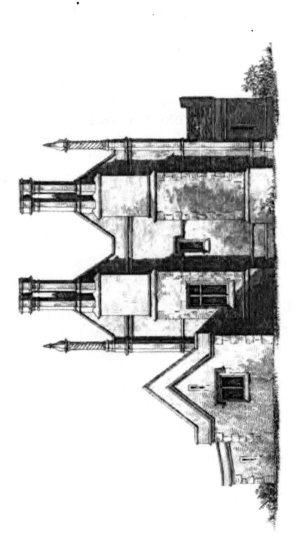

DESIGN Nº 5.

ORNAMENTAL VILLAS.

NEW SERIES.

DESIGN, No. III.

THIS building has recently been erected in Nottingham Park, upon the estate of the Duke of Newcastle. It contains an Entrance Hall, eight feet six inches square; a Staircase, fifteen feet by eight feet six inches; Dining Room, twenty feet by fifteen feet; a Drawing Room of the same size; and Library, fifteen feet square; Kitchen, Scullery, and Pantry, with five Rooms on the Chamber Story. It is a Villa upon a very small scale, and may be erected for £2,200.

Drawing Room

20'0 by 16'3

Library

16'0 Square

Dining Room

20'0 by 20'0

Staircase

Hall

Kitchen

Scullery

DESIGN N° 3.

Feet

DESIGN, N.º 3.

P.F.R. Arch.t

Scale of [   ] Feet.

Orn. Villas

DESIGN N.º 3.

Drawn by J.D Harding

Designed by H.N.H.

Printed by C. Hullmandel

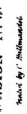

ORNAMENTAL VILLAS.

NEW SERIES.

DESIGN, No. IV.

THIS House was erected at Little Sampford in Essex for John Hinxman, Esq. It was destroyed by fire about two years since, and has not been rebuilt. It contained an Entrance Hall, two stories in height, twenty feet by sixteen feet six inches; a Staircase, twenty-three feet by sixteen feet six inches; Drawing Room, twenty-four feet by seventeen feet; Library, seventeen feet six inches by seventeen feet; Eating Room, twenty-four feet by seventeen feet; Gentleman's Room, Kitchen, Scullery, Larder, and Dairy; Servants' Hall, Laundry, and Footman's Closet, with five Bed Chambers, and five Servants' Rooms. The expense did not exceed £3,500.

SOUTH

DRAWING ROOM
24·0 X 17·0
12·0 HIGH

LIBRARY
17·0 SQUARE

DINING ROOM
24·0 X 17·0
12·0 HIGH

STAIRCASE
23·0 X 17·0

HALL
20·0 X 17·0

PORCH

OWN ROOM
17·0 X 12·0

W·C

HOUSEKEEPERS
ROOM
18·0 X 15·0

CLASS
CLOSET

E

W

DAIRY
10·0·0
DIAM

LARDER

PANTRY

KITCHEN
21·0 X 17·0

LAUNDRY
20·0 X 14·0

SERVANT'S
HALL
20·0 X 14·0

N

SCALE OF   FEET

PRINTED BY C. HULLMANDEL.

DESIGN N° 4.

J. P. R. ARCH.

Orn. Villas.

WEST FRONT.

SCALE OF

DESIGN, N°. 4.

P.F.R. ARCH.

PRINTED BY C.HULLMANDEL

Om Villas

EAST FRONT.

DESIGN Nº 4.

PRINTED BY C. HULLMANDEL

P.F.R. ARCH.

DESIGN Nº 4.

ORNAMENTAL VILLAS.

NEW SERIES.

DESIGN, No. V.

DUNSLEY Manor House is on Mr. Foley's estate, near Stourbridge. It is an ancient building, and has been used many years as a Farm House, but is now about to be made a Gentleman's residence. It will contain a Hall, nineteen feet by sixteen feet six inches; a Dining Room, seventeen feet six inches by fifteen feet; a Drawing Room, eighteen feet by fifteen feet; a Gentleman's Room, fourteen feet six inches by eleven feet; Kitchen, Scullery, Dairy, Larder, and Pantry, with four best Bed Chambers, and three rooms for Servants. The Plates, 18, 19, 20, will convey some idea of the external character proposed to be given to the building. A similar House might be erected for £3000.

Washhouse

Brewhouse

Office Court

Dairy

Scullery

Kitchen

Larder

Pantry

Breakfast Room

Hall

Own Room

Drawing Room

Porch

DESIGN No 3.

Scale of Feet

Ground Plan

Cott Villas

DESIGN No 6.

Scale of ...Feet

J.F.R. Arch.

WEST FRONT.

DESIGN Nº 6.

Drawn by J.D.Harding

DESIGN Nº 5.

Designed by T.F.H.

Printed by C. Hullmandel.

ORNAMENTAL VILLAS.

NEW SERIES.

DESIGN, No. VI.

THIS building is now in progress, and is situated on the shore of Swansea Bay, near Oystermouth. It will consist of an Entrance Porch, Staircase, fourteen feet six inches by ten feet six inches; a Dining Room, fourteen feet six inches square; a Drawing Room, twenty feet by fourteen feet six inches; a Gentleman's Room, nine feet by eight feet six inches; Store Room, Footman's Closet, Kitchen, Scullery, and Larder, with four Bed Chambers above, and four Rooms for Servants. The expense will not exceed £1,600.

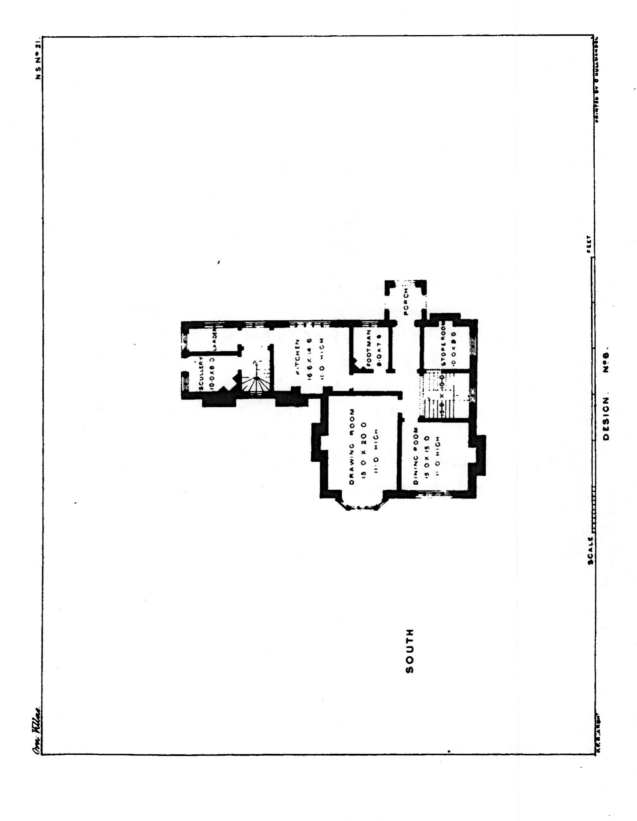

SOUTH

Orn. Villas.

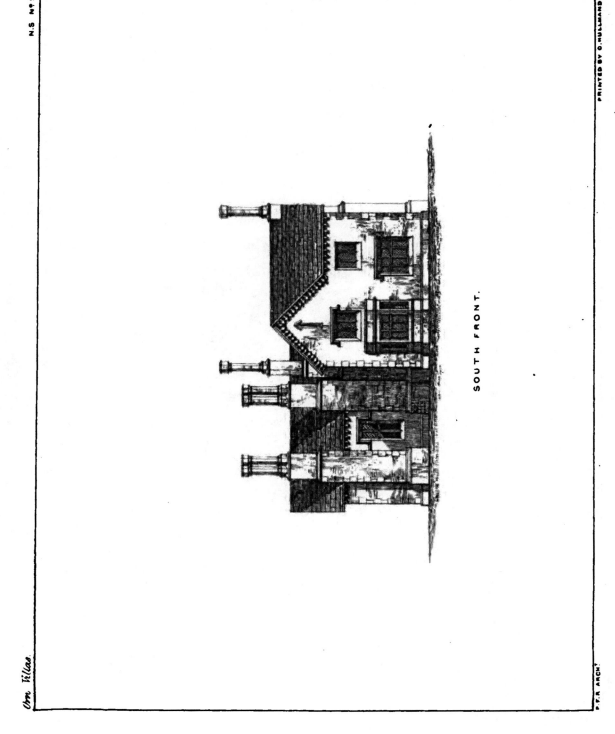

SOUTH FRONT.

DESIGN No 6.

PRINTED BY C.HULLMANDEL.

P.F.R ARCH.

Orn. Villas.

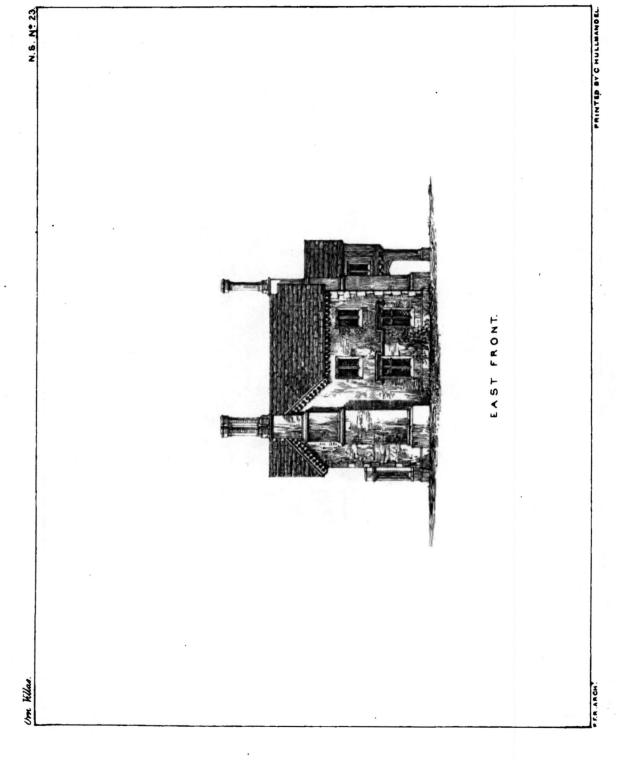

EAST FRONT.

P.F.R. ARCHT.

PRINTED BY C HULLMANDEL.

DESIGN Nº 6.

Drawn by J.D. Harding.

W. Walton, lithog.

Design by P.F.R.

DESIGN. No 3.

CPSIA information can be obtained at www.ICGtesting.com
Printed in the USA
BVOW06s1007100314

347178BV00007B/260/P